DEDICATION

This book is dedicated to three little girls who bring sunshine to our days and provide the inspiration for this effort. Our granddaughters, Delainey (Lainey), Lucy (Lu) and Harper (Harpy), are precious gifts from God.

When the time comes, I hope they will then pass this book on to their children.

Let me lie in your lap,
Let me ride on your knee.
Offer all of your kisses
to no one but me.

Hurry and hug me
and snuggle and smile.
I'll only be little
for a little while.
(author unknown)

INTRODUCTON

Many words, phrases and sayings have slowly passed out of our everyday usage. It's only when older folks, like myself, use them to illustrate a point that they resurface. We have three very young granddaughters, and I am often guilty of speaking a language totally foreign to them.

Things said that were common when I was a child traveled from generation to generation. I can still hear my grandmother saying, "Little pitchers have big ears," when adults were talking around the pinochle table and my brother and I were within earshot.

I thought it would be fun to write a series of short stories involving our granddaughters, using many of these old sayings. Some, I know, go back hundreds of years; others, I haven't a clue as to their original intent.

Some of the old-fashioned words or phrases within the context of the paragraph are self-explanatory. However, others will require some brief explanation. Hopefully, your young listeners will ask, "What's that mean?" Maybe it will rekindle fond memories from your own childhood.

OUR PAPA

TALKS FUNNY

by

Glenn Wyville

Illustrated by Dale Slavin

Windjammer Adventure Publishing
289 South Franklin Street, Chagrin Falls, OH 44022
Telephone 440.247.6610 Email windjammerpub@mac.com

TABLE OF CONTENTS

PAPA BABYSITS

The girls were excited. Papa would be over soon so Mom and Dad could go out for the evening.

"We'll be away till long after bedtime," announced Mom, "so Papa will be giving you supper, your bath and putting you to bed."

"What about stories?" asked Delainey.

"I'm sure he'll read some bedtime stories if you promise to stay in bed once you're tucked in," said Dad. "Grandma had to go to a meeting, so Papa will be *holding down the fort.*"

"What's a fort and why is Papa holding it down?" asked Lucy.

"It's like a castle you've heard about in the fairy tales I've read to you," explained Mom. "They lived in castles because they were safe there. A fort is the same thing."

The girls looked at one another with a puzzled expression. Neither had a clue as to what a fort was, much less, how to hold one down. A strange look appeared on Delainey's face.

"What's wrong?" asked Mom. "Don't you like to have Papa babysit you?"

"We do," shouted the girls in unison. That is, except for Harper, who couldn't talk yet. She just clapped her hands and jumped up and down, squealing with glee.

Delainey continued, "We always have fun when Papa comes over, but sometimes he says things I don't understand."

"Papa's a teaser," Lucy chimed in triumphantly.

"Grandpas are great teasers," said Mom, "and Papa is one of the best. Next time he says something you don't understand, just ask him what he means."

"He will often say things he heard when he was little like you girls," said Dad.

"Maybe *his* Papa was a teaser, too!" exclaimed Lucy.

"I can tell you for sure he was," said Dad. "Many of the things he says he heard as a little boy."

"Just think—someday you might be saying the same things to your children or grandchildren," said Mom.

At that very moment, the door opened and their grandfather stepped in.

"Papa, Papa," squealed the girls as they ran to him and wrapped their arms around each leg.

"Now that's what I call a *warm-hearted how-de-do*," said Papa as he picked up both girls and gave them a great big kiss. Meanwhile Harper, who was just beginning to walk, waddled over and reached upward with both arms, waiting for her turn. Delainey looked at Mom who gave her an approving nod.

"The girls want to know what a *warm-hearted how-de-do* means," said Mom. "They'll probably have a lot of other questions before they *hit the hay!*"

Don't you start too," said Dad. "One person talking funny is enough." They all laughed.

"I'll tell you what it means while we are having supper," said Papa. The table was set and dinner was ready so Mom and Dad kissed the girls and headed for the door.

"You girls be good and do as Papa says," cautioned Mom, as she stepped out the door.

After they all held hands and said grace, Delainey began her questioning again. "What's warm-hearted mean?" she asked.

"It's the opposite of cold-hearted," said Papa. "Which one do you think would mean being friendly?"

"I know," said Lucy. "It feels better to be warm than cold."

"Exactly," said Papa. "Your how-de-do or greeting made me feel good and warm all over."

As usual, Lucy was just picking at her food. She pushed her chair away, leaving a large portion of her supper untouched.

"Lucy," said Papa, "*you eat like a bird—hardly enough to keep a fly alive.*"

"What's that mean Papa?" asked Delainey.

"Well," said Papa, "I'm sure you've seen birds pick at seeds in your feeder. They don't get much in their little beaks."

"I'm not a bird," interrupted Lucy. "I'm a big girl!"

"No treats before bedtime unless you climb up and eat some more supper," said Papa. "Look at your sisters—they're almost finished. Good job, girls."

Lucy reluctantly climbed back up to the table and finished just enough to qualify for treats.

By the time everyone finished supper, it was nearly time for baths.

"Everyone upstairs. I'll get the bathwater ready," announced Papa. "Harper's ready for bed now, so I'll put a fresh diaper on and get her in her jammies. She'll be *snug as a bug in a rug*."

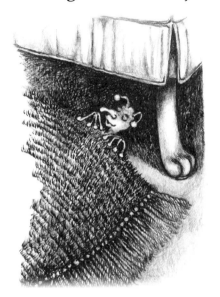

Papa saw the blank look on the girls' faces and knew he was going to have a good time tonight as the family teaser.

"What's that mean, Papa?" asked Delainey.

"It's just an old saying that means you'll be nice and warm and cozy," answered their grandfather.

"Why do they talk about bugs in their rugs?" Lucy was still puzzled.

"I think it means that a long time ago people didn't keep their homes as clean as they do today. In fact, when it got real cold outside, they would bring some of their barnyard animals indoors at night. Along with them came some bugs that were on the animals' fur. They would get in the rugs around the fireplace." Papa wasn't sure this was exactly what happened, but the girls seemed satisfied with his explanation.

"I'm going to see if Tillie brought any bugs in," said Lucy.

"Don't worry about Tillie," said Papa. "Her fur is too short—dogs won't carry bugs into the house. Anyway, it's time for baths, so hop in."

While the girls were splashing around in the tub, Papa decided to distract them enough in an attempt to keep most of the water in the tub.

"I'm going to read you a nursery rhyme if you'll sit quietly and just soak. Do you know what a nursery rhyme is?" asked Papa.

"It's a story before bedtime," said Delainey proudly.

"That's right, said Papa, "and the bedroom for children was called the nursery. We'll call this story a bathery rhyme." The girls giggled and splashed.

Opening an old, old book he brought from home, Papa said, "This is a book my grandma used to read from when I was your age. This bathery rhyme is called 'Wynken, Blynken and Nod' and it's about three children. It was written a long time ago by a man named Eugene Field. He loved little children just like I love you girls. Let's pretend it's Delainey, Lucy and Harper." Now he had the girls' full attention as he began to read:

WYNKEN, BLYNKEN AND NOD

Wynken, Blynken and Nod one night
Sailed off in a wooden shoe—
Sailed on a river of crystal light,

Into a sea of dew.
"Where are you going, and what do you wish?"
The old moon asked the three.
"We have come to fish for the herring fish
That live in this beautiful sea;
Nets of silver and gold have we!"
Said Wynken, Blynken, and Nod.

The old moon laughed and sang a song,
As they rocked in their wooden shoe,
And the wind that sped them all night long
Ruffled the waves of dew,
The little stars were the herring-fish
That lived in that beautiful sea—
"Now cast your nets wherever you wish—
But never afeared are we!"
So cried the stars to the fishermen three;
Wynken, Blynken, and Nod.

All night long their nets they threw
To the stars in the twinkling foam—
Then down from the skies came the wooden shoe,
Bringing the fishermen home;
"Twas all so pretty a sail, it seemed
As if it could not be,
And some folks thought 'twas a dream they dreamed
Of sailing that beautiful sea—
But I shall name you the fishermen three;
Wynken, Blynken, and Nod.

Wynken and Blynken are two little eyes,
And Nod is a little head,
And the wooden shoe that sailed the skies

Is a wee one's trundle-bed.
So shut your eyes while mother sings
Of wonderful sights that be,
And you shall see the beautiful things
As you rock on the misty sea,
Where the old shoe rocked the fishermen three;
Wynken, Blynken, and Nod.

When he had finished Delainey said, "That was a poem because the words rhymed."

"That's right," said Papa. "Nursery rhymes are bedtime stories that are sometimes poems."

"Can we hear another one?" asked Lucy.

"Of course," said Papa, "but you have to get your jammies on and crawl into bed. It's way past your bedtime. You have to promise not to *get up on the wrong side of the bed* in the morning and to be *bright-eyed and bushy-tailed* for Mama."

"What's that mean?" asked Delainey.

"Well," continued Papa, "it means to be cheerful in the morning. You can't be cross and whiney and you must do everything Mama asks."

"We promise," shouted the girls.

As soon as they were in bed, Papa reopened his old, old book. Before he began he said, "Let's say prayers first in case you fall asleep before I finish."

"O.K., Papa, it's a deal," said Delainey as the girls quietly said their evening prayers.

Papa sensed it wouldn't be much longer before the girls would be sailing off to Dreamland. He opened the old, old book and began reading:

WEE WILLIE WINKEY

Wee Willie Winkie

Runs through the town,

Upstairs and downstairs

In his night-gown,

Rapping at the window,

Crying through the lock,

"Are the children in their beds,

For now it's eight o'clock?"

His voice trailed off quietly as he finished. He smiled and softly closed the old, old book. His precious granddaughters were sound asleep.

TAKING A TRIP WITH GRANDMA AND PAPA

The girls' minds were racing. They were going to have more trouble than usual getting to sleep tonight. Early tomorrow Grandma and Papa would be over after breakfast. They were going to spend the day at the zoo.

Delainey tried to calm Lucy down. "Lu, the sooner we get to sleep the sooner morning will come. Remember, the same thing happened last Christmas. It seemed like Santa would never come because we were too excited to sleep."

"I don't remember, but if you say so…" said Lucy who didn't seem quite convinced.

Just then there was a loud noise outside the window. It was followed by a bright flash of light. Both girls sat straight up in bed as the room lit up like it was daylight. More thunder followed and then the rain started pounding on the window.

"Now we won't be able to go to the zoo tomorrow," said Delainey sadly.

"Oh, no!" Lucy started sobbing. Her big sister rushed over to her bed.

"Don't cry, Lu. It can't rain all night. I bet it'll be nice and clear by morning. It's better to be raining now than when we get up."

Delainey's words seemed to relieve Lucy's fears and she crawled back under the covers.

"It sure is nice to have a big sister that is so smart," thought

Lucy as she tried her best to get to sleep.

The next thing the girls knew, Dad was calling to them from the doorway.

"Better get up, girls. It's blueberry pancake time and they are hot off the griddle. Harper is up already and Mama is feeding her. I hope she hasn't eaten all the pancakes we made. It's *first come, first served* around here."

Blueberry pancakes were the girls' favorite, but there was something more important on their minds. They rushed to the window and were relieved to see bright shafts of sunlight coming through the trees.

"Hooray!" said Lucy. "You were right—now we can go to the zoo with Grandma and Papa. We'd better get downstairs before Harper eats all the pancakes."

"Don't worry, Lu. I'm sure Daddy will make more," said Delainey confidently.

Sure enough, Harper's cheeks were stuffed so full she looked like a chipmunk. As soon as Mom would put a piece of pancake on her tray, it was immediately stuffed into her already bulging cheeks.

"She's *happy as a clam at high tide*," said Dad.

Mom, Delainey and Lucy all looked at him at the same time.

"What's that mean?" they all said together.

"Well," said Dad, "clams are happy when the tide comes in. Then they are covered with a lot of water so people can't dig them up for food."

"Oh, I see," said Delainey hesitantly.

"I'm not a clam—I'm a big girl," said Lucy between bites of her pancakes.

"I'm not quite sure the girls made a connection with that one," said Mom. "Papa will definitely have some sayings they will understand better."

"Don't bet on it," said Dad as he finished off the last of the pancakes. "We need to get all that syrup off your hands and face before Grandma and Papa get here."

"What about Harper?" asked Lucy. "She even has syrup in her hair!"

This trip is just for us big girls," said Delainey proudly. "She's still a baby!!"

A few minutes later the girls' grandparents arrived.

"I was afraid we'd have to cancel our trip to the zoo," said Papa. "It was *raining cats and dogs* last night.

The girls looked at each other. "What's that mean, Papa?" asked Delainey.

"It's just an old saying that was used so long ago I'm not sure anybody remembers why it was said in the first place. Any time you hear it, that just means it was raining really, really hard," said Papa.

"That's good," said Delainey. "I'm glad no cats and dogs were falling from the sky."

"Me, too." said a very relieved Lucy. "They would get hurt if they fell from up so high."

"I'm glad we've settled that," said Dad. "Now you girls get into the car and remember to *mind your p's and q's* while you're with Grandma and Papa."

"Before you ask, Papa will tell you what it means while you're going to the zoo," said Mom.

As soon as they pulled out of the driveway, Delainey could no longer control herself. "What's *minding your p's and q's* mean?" she asked.

"Well," said Papa, "let me think. What comes after p?"

"Q," said Delainey immediately.

"Right you are," said Papa. "You were paying attention to what I said and that means you were listening. When my Mama told me to *mind my p's and q's* I knew I had to listen to what I was told and to be on my best behavior. But we don't have to worry about that—you girls always *mind your p's and q's.*"

"I'll even mind my *abc's*," said Lucy proudly.

Everyone laughed as they headed off for a fun day at the zoo.

ON TO THE ZOO

Delainey asked, "Are we there yet?" as the car slowed down at a traffic light. *"Hold your horses,"* said Papa. "We'll be there before you can say *'Jack Robinson'."*

"What?" asked Lucy. "We don't have any horses and who's

Jack Robinson?" asked Delainey. "Papa, you're such a teaser."

"What Papa means is that you need to be patient and we'll be there soon," said Grandma. "When you hold your horses you don't have to be in such a hurry. You're moving too fast—you need to slow down and be patient. And Jack Robinson is just a long word meaning we'll be there before you can say it."

"Jack Robinson…." said Lucy. "I don't see the zoo."

"Be patient," said Papa as they turned down a road that had a big sign—ZOO!!

"Hooray!" said Grandma. "Now I don't have to explain any more sayings for now."

They were directed to the parking lot and soon after, were walking through the entrance to the zoo.

"What do you want to see first?" asked Grandma.

Just then a huge bird walked in front of them and spread its colorful tail feathers out like a giant fan. The girls stopped in their tracks.

Lucy jumped behind Delainey and peered out cautiously.

"Don't be afraid, Lu," assured Delainey. "Don't you remember? It's one of the animals on our Go Fish game cards. It's a peacock!"

"Very good, Delainey," said Papa. "You make me feel *proud as a peacock* when you show how much you've learned. Now you can see how that saying came about. He looks pretty proud, walking around with his bright tail feathers spread out."

"Let's walk over to Monkey Island. It's always fun to watch them play," said Grandma.

Soon they were standing at the railing watching a funny show. The monkeys were scampering about, picking up objects and studying them. Some were chasing others around the island, up and down the small hills and out on the limbs of trees. Some were climbing up ropes and swinging on car tires. Mother monkeys were carrying their tiny babies around on their backs. A large crowd had gathered and everyone was enjoying the show.

"They're having *more fun than a barrel of monkeys*," exclaimed Grandpa.

The girls didn't need to have an explanation. They only had to watch the goings-on all over the island to understand this saying.

"Can't they get out?" asked Delainey.

"They don't like to swim in the water that's around the island," said Papa. "They are not good swimmers. Then they have to try to climb the steep cliff to where we are standing. Besides, they are having too much fun to want to leave."

"We could watch them *until the cows come home,*" said Papa, grinning.

"What?" asked the girls.

"On, no!" said Grandma. "Here we go again. It just means that we would be here a long time. The cows on the farm don't come to the barn from grazing in the pasture until late in the day."

"I know," said Delainey. "It's another old saying from Papa, the teaser."

"And it's still early in the day," groaned Grandma.

"We'd better hurry if you want to see the whole *kit and caboodle*," said Papa as he hurried up a path before the girls could say, "What's that?"

"I guess Papa is hurrying up the path because he is in a rush and wants to see everything," said Delainey.

"Very good," said Grandma. "You seem to be catching on to Papa's funny talk. Sometimes *I* don't even know what he's talking about."

A loud roar grabbed the girls' attention. Not more than ten feet away, behind tall, thick bars, a huge lion paced back and forth.

"I'm scared," said Delainey.

"M-e-e-e-e too," said Lucy.

"Don't worry. We're safe here," assured Grandma. "He's just showing off for us. Anyway, he couldn't get out if he wanted to."

"Don't worry, girls," said Papa confidently. *"His bark is worse than his bite.* He's just a big, cowardly lion—you know, like in the Wizard of Oz."

Delainey said, "I usually believe what you say, but not this time. Look at those giant teeth!"

"You're right," said Grandma. "Sometimes you need to let what Papa says *go in one ear and out the other.*"

"That's because he's a teaser," said Lucy.

"You're right, girls," said Papa. "I was just trying to stop you from being afraid. A zoo is a very safe place; otherwise, no one would come here."

As they continued along the path they passed cages with

tigers, leopards and other large cat-like animals.

"I'm not afraid anymore," said Delainey, confidently. "They are here for us to enjoy."

Yeah," said Lucy. "We only get to see them in books and on T.V. I'm having *more fun than a barrel of monkeys.*"

Everyone laughed as Lucy stood there, grinning from ear to ear.

"I think it's about time we had something to eat," said Papa. "I'm so hungry I could eat a skunk."

"I'm so hungry I could eat an elephant," said Delainey.

"I'm so hungry I could eat a whale," exclaimed Lucy.

"I think you'll all have to settle for hot dogs and French fries," said Grandma. "Skunks, elephants and whales will have to wait for another time."

"What do you want to *wet your whistle?*" asked Papa.

"I know what that means," said Delainey, proudly. "If my mouth was too dry I wouldn't be able to whistle. I'll have milk please."

"Me, too," said Lucy, "only I don't know how to whistle."

"I think the girls are catching on to your silly sayings," said Grandma.

"I've got plenty more that they haven't heard yet," said Papa as he left to get the food. When he returned everyone ate quickly because there was still much to see.

"We'd better *get the lead out of our feet*," said Papa. "We'll have to come back another day because we won't have time to visit every *nook and cranny*," he said as he gathered up all the trash and hurried off to the trash barrel.

"Oh, no!" said Grandma. *"He left me holding the bag.* I'm stuck explaining this."

"What Papa means is we'd better hurry and not move like our feet are made of heavy lead. Then we won't have time to go everywhere and see everything."

The girls seemed satisfied when their grandpa returned.

"Grandma, you're getting to be a *chip off the old block*," said Papa. "You explained things just right. Now the girls will be worried that you'll be talking funny like me."

"I'll never be able to explain all your sayings," said Grandma, "but I guess I told them enough to satisfy the girls' curiosity."

As they visited more areas of the zoo they saw elephants, giraffes and hippos. There were birds of every color and seals splashing in the water, turning on their backs and clapping their flippers together. After awhile the girls were starting to show the effects of a long day.

"We'd *better head for the barn*," said Papa. "The girls seem to have lost their *pep and vinegar*. I'm getting a little *tuckered out* myself."

"We don't live in a barn," corrected Lucy, "we live in a house."

"It just means the same thing, but the farmers went to their animals' home to put them to bed for the night," explained Grandma.

"Yes," said Papa, "I can see you girls are not quite as peppy as you were. It's been a long, fun day and we are all getting tired."

"Can we come back another day?" asked Lucy.

"Of course," said Grandma. "We didn't see everything. We only *scratched the surface* today." The girls were too tired to ask what that meant.

After strapping the girls in their car seats, they were headed for home.

"Thanks for the fun day, Grandma and Papa," said Delainey. "We sure liked coming to the zoo with you."

"Even if you do talk funny," added Lucy.

Papa looked in the rear view mirror and before he could answer, both girls were *out like a light*.

FEEDING GOLDFISH AT PAPA'S POND

It was a beautiful early summer day. After breakfast Mama packed lunches for everyone, and they all headed up the hill to the Rec Center. It was a long walk so they planned on stopping at Grandma and Papa's house for a little rest and some welcome refreshments.

When they reached Grandma and Papa's house Lucy was bringing up the rear, as usual.

"Oh, I guess you didn't bring Lucy today," said Papa, pretending not to see her as she slowly approached the driveway.

"She's with us," Delainey informed him. "Lu's her usual slowpoke self."

"Lucy's *slower than molasses in January,*" said Papa.

"What is molasses?" asked Delainey.

"Well," said Papa, "molasses is like syrup you put on your blueberry pancakes. What do you think would happen if you put syrup outside in the winter?"

"It would freeze and we couldn't pour it on our blueberry pancakes," she informed him.

"Right," said Papa. "Sort of like your sister. She moves slowly, just like molasses in January. Now let's go out to the pond while your Mama goes in to *chew the fat* with Grandma."

"What are they going to chew on?" asked Lucy who had finally caught up.

"It means they sit down and talk a lot," said Grandpa. "You know—they *beat their gums* and talk about everything *from soup to nuts.*"

Delainey was anxious to change the subject so she could go out to feed the fish, but Lucy was still curious about what Papa had just said.

"Wouldn't it hurt if they beat their gums while they're eating soup and nuts?" asked Lucy.

"Don't worry," said Papa. "Beating their gums just means they're talking a lot about *everything under the sun.*"

By this time Delainey was already standing near the edge of the small pond in the backyard. Papa poured a small amount of fish food in her hands and she tossed it out into the center.

Now it was Lucy's turn as he poured some fish food in her hand.

"Make sure you toss it out far enough so that it reaches the water," said Papa. Sometimes their fish food ended up in the flower beds.

"I can't see any fish. Can you turn the fountain off?" asked Delainey. Papa entered the garage and pulled the plug on the fountain's pump.

"I'll bet you can see fish now," said Papa.

"There they are!" said Lucy excitedly. "They were hiding in the weeds."

"They wait until *the coast is clear,* then dart out *quick as a bunny,*" said Papa.

The girls had a slight idea of what he was talking about, but were still confused.

"The goldfish are playing hide and seek with us," said Delainey. "When they think it's safe, they come out."

"Very good," said Papa. "We're so big and they're so small. I think we'd be afraid, too, if the fish were bigger than us."

"Let's *mosey*, I mean go inside, and feast our eyes on the treats that Grandma has made for us."

The girls knew exactly what he was talking about and scampered behind him, knowing something delicious was waiting in the kitchen.

THE LONG HIKE

Grandma and Papa decided they would go with Mama and the girls on the long hike up the hill for a fun day at the Rec Center. Lunches and snacks had been packed along with bathing suits, towels, books and toys. It would be a long day and Daddy was going to meet them later in the afternoon for a swim, dinner and a ride home.

"I love the Rec Center," said Delainey. "It's so much fun and there's a lot to do."

The Rec Center was the main destination for summer fun in the Village. Children and their parents from all over the area enjoyed the pools, tennis courts, ballfields and game room.

Delainey and Lucy were excited because they would be taking their swimming lessons. Harper was still too young, but she would be content splashing around in the baby pool.

"You girls are going to be as *busy as a bees,*" said Papa as they climbed into the wagon.

Harper was securely strapped into the stroller and they were off on their long hike.

"We're not bees, we're little girls," said Lucy.

"No, but we'll be busy like bees today," said Delainey. "It's just another of Papa's funny sayings."

"It's a long way up to the Rec Center, and if we don't hurry we'll never make it in time for your swimming lessons," said Papa.

"Oh, no!" sighed the girls.

"We know it's a long way so we'd better get going," added Delainey. "The guards are testing us today and if we pass, they hand out treats."

"Don't get *down in the mouth,* girls. If we *don't beat around the bush* I'm sure we'll get there in plenty of time," Papa assured them.

"Better tell the girls what you mean," said Mama, as they started the long hike up the hill.

"Well," Papa started, "when you're not happy, your mouth curls down at the corners like this." Papa demonstrated an extra sad face. "When you *beat around the bush* it means you are not going straight to where you want to go so it takes longer."

"We don't want to do that," said Lucy. "I want a treat so I guess we all need to hurry."

The girls arrived in time, changed into their swimming suits and entered the pool for their lessons. A short time later Delainey came rushing over, holding a large cookie covered with pink icing.

"Looks like you *came through with flying colors,*" said Papa.

Just then Lucy appeared with her towel draped over her head. There was no cookie in her hand and she sat on a bench with her back to everyone. Delainey walked over and sat down beside her unhappy sister and gave her a big hug. Then both girls turned and walked toward their mama. Their faces were beaming and each held half of a cookie with pink icing.

"You're a *good egg,*" said Papa. "I always knew you had a *heart of gold* and we're all very proud of you. A little bird must have told you that Lucy needed a *shot in the arm.*"

"Lucy's not sick," said

Delainey. "I gave her a cookie—not medicine."

"Yes," said Papa, "but your cookie treat perked her up, just like medicine, and made her feel good."

Both girls sat on the bench and enjoyed Delaney's gift of good medicine.

"You're a *good egg,*" said Lucy. "Did a bird really tell you to share your cookie with me?"

Harper saw them eating cookies and scrambled out of the baby pool. She rushed over with her arms outstretched saying, "Cookie, Cookie!" Each girl broke off a piece of their cookie and gave it to Harper, who eagerly stuffed it into her mouth.

"Being generous is a good trait to have," said Grandma, "and we're happy you gave Harper some of your cookie."

"I know w*e put the cart before the horse,*" said Papa.

I hope you all still have room for lunch in your tummies.

What Grandma made is guaranteed to *make your mouth water*."

"Papa," said Delainey, standing in front of her grandfather with her hands on her hips. "That's silly! Whoever heard of the cart in front and the horse in back?"

"Papa just means we gave you your dessert first instead of after lunch. It was in the wrong order," explained the girls' mother. "We hope you won't *turn up your nose* at the nice lunch Grandma fixed for you. She'll feel bad if you don't eat it."

The girls sat patiently at the picnic table as Grandma placed a tasty sandwich and juice box in front of them.

"I'm glad to see your *eyes weren't bigger than your stomachs*," said Papa as the girls eagerly devoured their sandwiches and gulped down their juice.

"Since you left more room in your stomachs, I think we have some dessert left for you," said Grandma.

"I'm sure this will *stick to your ribs*," said Papa as Grandma gave each of them a slice of berry pie.

"I don't want this pie sticking to my ribs," said Lucy. "I want it sticking in my tummy."

"It just means that it is very good to eat, and don't worry—it will end up in the right place," explained Grandma.

After lunch Delainey and Lucy walked over to the middle pool with their mama. Harper remained at the baby pool to splash around with Grandma and Papa.

Later that afternoon Daddy appeared at the fence and called

to the girls. They rushed over to greet him and Papa brought Harper from the baby pool.

"I have to tell you about the nice thing Delainey and Lucy did today," said Papa. He told their dad about their cookie sharing.

"You girls are so generous," Dad exclaimed. "You make me feel *proud as a peacock.*"

"We know what that means," they shouted. "Papa told us the funny saying about proud peacocks the day we went to the zoo."

BACKYARD VISITORS

Papa was sitting with the girls at their picnic table having a morning snack of milk and cookies. Even though it was still winter they were outside because it was a very warm day. The ground was covered with snow, but they were enjoying the feel of sunshine on their faces.

Suddenly they heard a loud noise coming from the woods along the creek bank. Papa pointed to a row of trees at the bottom of the sled-riding hill and then put his finger to his lips. The girls became very quiet and slowly turned their heads in that direction. A large deer poked its head out from the woods at the edge of the lawn.

"You have to be *quiet as a church mouse* or you'll *spook them* and they'll *high-tail it*," whispered Papa.

The girls were tempted to ask where the church mice and spooks were hiding but remained silent.

Delainey couldn't stand it any longer, and since she was sitting next to Papa she whispered in his ear. "Mama said I could ask you when you say something we don't understand. Lucy and I want to know what you mean."

"Lean closer, girls," said Papa quietly. "I can't talk loudly because I don't want to spook, I mean scare them."

The girls moved closer so Papa could speak very quietly.

He whispered, "I'll bet you never saw a mouse in church."

"I never did," said Delainey.

"I never heard one either," chimed in Lucy.

"That's because they creep around so quietly you'd never know they were around," said Papa.

"What's a high tail have to do with it?" asked Lucy.

"Well," said Papa, "when big animals like deer run away, their tails fly up behind them. So you see, everything I say has a special meaning if you think about it. Now, if we aren't quiet, all we might see is their tails as they run back into the woods."

The deer looked carefully in all directions, making sure it was clear and then slowly stepped out in the open.

Still whispering, Papa said, "They may act like they have *eyes in the back of their heads* and can see in every direction, but they can hear us easier than they can see us. In the winter food is scarce so they have to *look high and low* and can't be *persnickety* or choosy.

Often they come right out in the open if they think there is food. If we stay very quiet, we may see a deer parade."

The girls seemed satisfied with Papa's explanation and returned their attention to the deer.

No sooner had he spoken than a second deer, larger than the other, stepped out from the woods. Soon three more deer, much smaller than the others, stepped slowly out in the open.

"Those are their babies from last year," said Papa. "They are called yearlings because they are about one year old."

They all began pawing away the snow with their hooves and nibbling the grass underneath. Every few seconds the larger deer would raise its head, look around and twitch its big ears.

"They are always *on pins and needles*, which means nervous, when they are out in the open like this and have to be very alert."

Even Papa's low whisper caused them to stop eating and look in all directions.

"Papa," said Lucy in a loud voice, "they better not come up the hill and start eating our pasta." (Lucy called the hosta plants, pasta).

That was all it took. In a twinkling of an eye, all they saw were white tails pointing to the sky as they quickly vanished into the woods.

"Now look what you've done, Lu," scolded Delainey. "You spoiled our deer parade." Lucy began to curl her lower lip and was nearly in tears. Delainey walked over to her little sister and gave her a warm hug.

"Don't be sad, Lu. We'll have a deer parade every day now that they know we have such tasty grass."

"That's right," assured Papa. "If you *keep your eyes pealed* and stay *quiet as a church mouse*, there will be many more backyard visitors."

"I sure hope they stay out of our pasta," said Lucy as the girls went back to enjoying their morning snack in the warm sunshine—but not before there was one more question.

"Papa," asked Delainey, "how do we peal our eyes?"

Papa laughed and looked at them with eyes so wide open that they looked like they were about to pop out of his head. The girls looked at one another the same way and began laughing along with Papa.

"Now we all have pealed eyes," said Lucy.

A WALK UP TOWN

It was a bright, sunny day and Harper was taking her afternoon nap, so Papa decided it would be a good time for the girls and him to hike up town.

"We'll take the little red wagon in case you girls get *all tuckered out*." he said. "Grandma is a little *under the weather* so it's just the three of us."

"What's that mean?" asked Delainey.

"Which one—*all tuckered out* or *under the weather*?" asked Papa.

"Both of them," said Lucy.

"Well," continued Papa, "if you're *all tuckered out*, it's just an old-fashioned way of saying you are getting tired out and need a rest. And Grandma isn't feeling well and she is no *spring chicken*. Besides, someone has to stay home with Harper while she naps."

"Papa," said Delainey with her hands on her hips, "Grandma is not a chicken! She's younger than you, so you must be an old rooster."

Lucy chimed in, "Yeah, you're an old teaser too."

Papa laughed. "Come on, pile in the red wagon and I'll explain what I meant on our way up town."

The girls hopped in as Papa continued.

"*Under the weather* goes way back to the days when all ships only used sails, so ocean trips took a long time. When there was a storm on the water, people often got sick because the small boat bounced around. They would then go down below the ship's deck. So they were then *under the weather*."

"How can you be a chicken if you're a person?" asked Delainey.

"Grandma is not a *spring chicken* because chicken's eggs hatch in the spring, so it means a *spring chicken* is very young," explained Grandpa.

"Like Harper, but not like Grandma," said Lucy.

"So I guess she's not a *spring chicken* after all," said Papa. "I wonder if *Grandma's ears are burning?*" he asked.

"What?" exclaimed Lucy. "Why are Grandma's ears on fire? Will her ears get burned?"

"Don't worry," Papa assured them. "It just means someone is talking about them when they're not around."

"I guess it's just Papa talking silly again," said Delainey.

They were passing some beautiful old homes and were nearly up to the Methodist Church at the edge of town.

"Our town is *pretty as a picture*," said Papa. "Everyone who comes here has to stop at the falls and visit all the nice shops."

"And stop for ice cream at the Popcorn Shop," said Delainey eagerly.

"Are we going to stop at the Popcorn shop?" asked Lucy.

Just as Papa was about to answer, a lady approached and greeted him.

"These must be your granddaughters," she said. "My sakes alive, they're just as *cute as a bunny*. I can see why they are the *apple of your eye*."

"Yes, they are," said Papa, as he broke into a big smile, "and they're *sweeter than fresh cider* to boot."

Now the girls were thoroughly confused. "Papa, I thought you were the only one who talked funny," whispered Delainey. "Do all your friends who are old people talk that way?" She spoke quietly fearing she would hurt the lady's feelings.

"Since these are old sayings, I guess you can say that's true," Papa continued. "I think little bunnies are very cute, don't you? And you sure are the apple of my eye because you always make me so happy, just like eating a good apple. Next fall I'll give you some sweet apple cider and you'll know what I mean."

"I guess that they are saying nice things about us, Lu," said Delainey. "I'm not just exactly sure what they mean though. Maybe when we get as old as Papa, we'll talk funny too."

As they continued through the village, several people they passed greeted their grandpa.

"Papa, you must know everybody in town," said Lucy. "Are you a famous person?

"Not really," said Papa. "I'm more like *a big frog in a small pond*."

Before they could ask what he meant, a lady approached who recognized the girls.

"Why Delainey and Lucy, it's so nice to see you. Who is this pulling you through town"?

"This is our Papa," said Delainey proudly.

"He's *a big frog in a small pond*," added Lucy, not really knowing what she was saying.

The lady laughed and their grandpa stood there looking *red as a beet*. Papa was very embarrassed by Lucy's remark and tried to explain why he said he was a frog.

"I guess if you live in a small town long enough, you get to know just about everyone. Sort of like all the animals knowing a big frog lives in their small pond."

"Oh, I see," said the lady politely. She appeared as confused as the girls by this comparison.

Papa gave a sigh of relief as they continued on their way. Nearing the bridge over the falls the girls immediately recognized their favorite spot—the Popcorn Shop! As usual Papa, the teaser, looked the other way, pretending not to notice.

"Papa, Papa, can't we stop, please?" the girls pleaded.

"Oh, you want to stop and look at the falls?" asked Papa with a grin. "Sure we can, but there's a better view on the other side of the bridge."

"No, no, we mean the Popcorn Shop. Can't we get some ice cream?" the girls begged.

"What's the magic word?" asked Papa.

"Pleeeese!" screamed the girls in one loud voice.

"Who put *a bee in your bonnet* about stopping for ice cream?" asked Papa. "Did anybody bring money?"

The girls looked at each other as disappointment crept across their faces.

"We don't have any *bees in our bonnets*

or any money for ice cream either," said Lucy sadly.

"I just mean who gave you that idea?" said Papa. "I guess we can go in but you have to promise to eat a good lunch for Grandma."

"We promise," said the girls as they scrambled out of the red wagon and ran for the door.

Then Papa reached in his pocket and pulled out his wallet.

"I might have enough in here for two little girls who are as cute as bunnies and sweet as fresh apple cider," said Papa.

Their faces brightened as they bounded through the door of the Popcorn Shop. Delainey stopped and looked back as they entered.

"Papa, you're such a teaser!" she exclaimed.

A VISIT TO THE OLD HARDWARE

After finishing the tasty treat at the Popcorn Shop, Papa decided there was enough time for a couple more stops before heading home.

"Hop in the wagon, girls," he said. "We're going to visit my friends at the old hardware. They continued up to the next corner and started across Main Street at the crosswalk.

"Papa, watchout!" screamed Lucy. "There are cars coming both ways."

"Don't worry girls," he assured them. "When they see us starting to cross, we expect them to stop, but you have to double check before stepping in the street. That post in the middle of the street means "STOP" and let walkers cross. People are very polite about walkers, and you can wave to them to say thank you for stopping."

The girls felt very grown up waving to the cars and were especially pleased when the drivers waved back.

"Big Mike", the U.P.S. driver, even stuck his arm out of his brown truck, beeped his horn and gave the girls a thumbs up.

As they reached the curb Delainey saw they were right next to the park.

"Papa, can we go to the park and feed the ducks?" she asked.

"Sure," said her grandpa, "but we'll have to go to the old hardware first. They have the best duck food in town and even have lollypops for good little girls and boys."

"Is that true?" questioned Lucy, "or are you just teasing again?"

"Trust me," said Papa, "they have *everything but the kitchen sink* inside."

As they entered they were met at the door by a man with a white beard wearing blue bib overalls.

"Say hello to Rob, girls," said Papa. "He's a *Jack of all trades* and the *chief cook and bottle washer* around here."

"Hello Mr. Rob," said Delainey. "I don't understand how you can cook and wash bottles here if you don't even have a kitchen sink."

Rob looked a bit puzzled by Delainey's question.

"Our Papa is a teaser," said Lucy. "He is always saying funny things."

"What I mean, girls, is if you have a question about how something works or how to fix a *thing-a-ma-jig*, Rob can usually put you *on the right track*," said Papa. "Today we have come for your finest duck food and maybe lollypops for two little girls who have been very good today."

"Fine with me," said Rob as he winked at their grandpa, "but you have to ask the old troll who lives in a dark corner in the back of the store. He goes by the name of Jack."

The girls looked nervously at Papa.

"Will Jack the troll bite us if we get too close?" asked Lucy.

"Not to worry," said Rob. "Jack is an old troll and all his teeth have fallen out long ago. He might just gum you a little bit."

The girls were quite nervous as they walked slowly behind their grandpa and headed for the counter in the back of the store. They were expecting Jack the fearsome troll to jump out at any second. To their relief, they were greeted by a smiling lady behind the counter.

"Hi girls," said the lady. "I bet your grandpa brought you in for an official Chagrin Hardware lollypop."

"Hi Sue," said Papa. "Right you are, but we also need some of your equally famous duck food."

The girls were still looking in all directions. Each aisle was crowded with many unusual things and hiding places. There were strange noises that seemed to be coming from every part of the store.

Just then a large dog came around the corner, followed by a little old lady wearing a huge sun bonnet. The dog was right in Lucy's face and began licking her.

"Stop it, Brutus," she commanded in a high-pitched voice. "The little girl doesn't want any dog kisses." She pulled hard on the leash.

"Sorry, dearie. Brutus must be after the ice cream on your face."

Although Lucy was frightened at first, she was relieved that it wasn't Jack the Troll gumming her.

After giving Brutus his milk bone treat, Sue brought out a tall jar filled with lollypops of every color.

"I'll bet you girls would like one of these," she said.

"Yes, please," said Delainey, almost in a whisper. "Is Jack the toothless troll hiding somewhere back here?"

Sue burst out laughing as she reached into the jar. "I've never heard him called that, but some of our customers have called him an ogre from time to time. Did your grandpa tell you that?"

Just then, a loud laugh coming from the front of the store told her who was guilty of the prank.

"I might have known," she said. "Another of Rob's jokes. Sometimes he stands next to the wooden Indian and pretends to be ducking away from his hatchet."

Still not sure it was safe, Lucy's hand reached slowly from behind her sister for the treat.

"Here's Jack the troll now," announced Sue between laughs. The girls quickly jumped behind their grandpa and slowly peeked out.

"I hear Rob's been *telling some tall tale*s about me," Jack said as he smiled down at the girls.

"Look Lu," said Delainey. "He has all his teeth and seems like a nice man."

"I guess Mr. Rob is a teaser like Papa," said Lucy.

Jack shook their hands and placed another lollypop in each girl's palm.

"Thank you, Mr. Jack," said Delainey. "We're glad you're not a troll or an ogre."

"Come on girls," said Papa. "We can't *dilly-dally* or we won't have time to feed the ducks."

"What's a dilly?" asked Lucy.

"And what's a dally?" added Delainey. "Why won't dilly-dallying let us feed the ducks?"

"Well," said Papa, "it means we can't waste time or we'll be late for lunch and Grandma will be *madder than a wet hen*."

"Grandma's not a chicken, Papa," said Lucy. "You're teasing us again."

"I know," said Papa. "Chickens don't like to get wet and they get mad when you dump water on them. Grandma will be mad if she has lunch ready and we don't show up."

"Let's hurry over to the river so Grandma doesn't turn into a wet hen," said Delainey as she ran toward the back door of the hardware store.

FEEDING THE DUCKS AND SOME UNWANTED GUESTS

Papa and the girls passed through the store on their way out the back door. Delainey and Lucy were still a little nervous, especially when they saw some of the unusual objects stored in the rear of the store. As they headed out the hardware door Papa had a question for them.

"Do you girls realize how lucky you are to have a special hardware like this and a river running right through your town? You are extra lucky to have a waterfalls to boot. Not many towns *can hang their hats on that.*"

"Papa," said Delainey, "I'd like to see you hang your hat on a waterfall."

The girls were now more interested in feeding the ducks than Papa's old sayings so they didn't question his latest funny saying. Instead, they ran toward the river. Each had a small bag of duck food. As they approached, the ducks seemed to sense a treat was in store for them. Some climbed out of the water and waddled closer. Others remained in the river, circling around near the bank. They knew that some tasty morsels would soon be thrown their way.

The girls tossed food which was easily picked up by those closest to them on the shore. The ducks were racing through the water to be the first to reach the tiny bits of bread they had thrown.

"That just goes to show," said Papa, "that *the early bird gets the worm* every time."

"We're not feeding them worms," said Lucy, "and those are ducks, not birds."

Just as their grandpa was about to get into a lesson about ducks really being a kind of bird, the ducks began quacking loudly. Something had scared them and they rushed back into the water without looking back or finishing the rest of the delicious meal.

"Look Papa," said Delainey. "I see what scared them."

The girls jumped behind their grandpa as three large black and white geese rushed over from across the lawn. They began honking loudly and their long necks were sticking almost straight out. Papa stepped toward them as they began to greedily eat the duck food.

"*Skeedaddle* you *scallywags*!" he shouted.

The girls had a faint idea that he was scolding them because the geese stopped dead in their tracks. They didn't back away, however, and began honking even louder as they flapped their large wings, showing their displeasure.

"Wild animals always get *riled up* when you try to take their food away," said Papa. "These *bad eggs* are just trying to put on a show.

"They don't look like eggs to me," said Lucy.

"It's just a term for someone who is not being nice," said Papa. "Did you ever smell a *bad egg*?"

"I did," said Delainey. "Pee-uh!"

"They think they can scare us, but *their bark is worse than their bite.*"

"Their honk may be worse than their bite, but I don't want to find out," said Delainey. "Let's let them stay in charge here and move down toward the playground, pleeeeeese!"

Lucy was too afraid to talk, but she shook her head in total agreement with her sister.

"Come on, girls, we'll *give them a wide berth*," said Papa.

They circled out on the lawn, far from the honking geese. The girls ran ahead while keeping a watchful eye on the noisy intruders. They were so concerned that they hadn't noticed the ducks paddling right along with them.

"I hope you have some duck treats left," announced Papa. "Look in the water. Now you can go to the bank and toss the rest of the food out to them." They were pleased to see a group of ducks eagerly waiting as they approached the playground.

The girls had a great time watching the ducks paddle around, bobbing their heads under the water to gather the food the girls had tossed out.

When the food was gone, Papa said, "You know what to do with the empty bag, and then we have a little time for the playground."

The girls rushed over to the trash container and then ran to the playground. Their grandpa followed pulling the red wagon. He watched the girls scampering up the ladder and riding the slide down time after time.

"Papa," they shouted, "we're having more fun than a barrel of monkeys like the ones we saw at the zoo."

"I wish I had that much energy," thought Papa. "They're making me tired and they have to be starting to wind down too. I have a feeling that this wagon is going to come in handy on the way home."

A short time later their grandpa called to the girls. "Time to *shake a leg* and head for home."

Delainey and Lucy were slowly getting used to some of the funny sayings and started shaking their legs and laughing. They quickly jumped into the wagon as Papa strapped them in.

"Thanks for bringing us up town today. It was fun in spite of the *bad eggs*," said Delainey.

"I didn't smell any *bad eggs* and where were the early birds?" asked Lucy.

"I'm going to give you a riddle to think about on the way

home," said Papa. "Get ready! All ducks are birds, but not all birds are ducks."

When they reached the park's end and entered the sidewalk on Main Street their grandpa looked back at them for an answer to the riddle. He smiled and began again gently pulling the wagon. The answer would have to wait. They were now dreaming about all the fun things that happened on the trip to town.

BUSHY-TAILED THIEVES

One morning Papa appeared with a homemade birdfeeder. Now the girls could watch them eating right from their kitchen window. He hung it from a hook on a nearby tree and filled it with seeds.

"If you sit here, even on the coldest days, you can enjoy a *feast for your eyes* while the birds are enjoying a feast for their tummies," said Papa.

"I can't wait for the birds to come," said Delainey excitedly. "What kind will we see?"

"It will bring a lot of different kinds because we use black oil sunflower seeds. They are the favorite snack for most birds. The trouble is, there is someone else who likes those seeds too," cautioned Papa. "Let me read you a little poem and see if you can guess who it is." He opened up the old book of nursery rhymes and began to read:

Whisky, Frisky,
Hippity Hop,
Up He Goes
To the Tree Top!

Furly, Curly,
What a Tail!
Tall as a Feather,
Broad as a Sail!

Whirly, Twirly,
Round and Round,
Down He Scampers
To the Ground.

Where's His Supper?
In the Shell;
Snappy, Cracky,
Out it Fell!

"I know," shouted Lucy.

"I know who it is, too," echoed Delainey.

"How about this?" said Papa. "I'll count to three and you can both give me the answer together. One, Two, Three!"

"Mr. Squirrel!!" they shouted.

"Very good girls," said Papa. "That bushy-tailed thief will sneak up and empty the seed tray *clean as a whistle*."

"What's a clean whistle?" asked Lucy.

"I know," chimed in Delainey. "Listen to me whistle and you'll hear how clear it is and then how fast it's gone." Delainey had just learned to whistle and was very proud of her new skill.

"When it comes to knowing how to steal food, they are *at the head of the class,*" said Papa, "because they are *smart as a whip* and no matter how hard you try to outsmart them, they dig into their *bag of tricks* and get more seeds than the birds."

"What?" said Delainey. "Trying to understand your funny sayings is almost as hard as outsmarting Mr. Squirrel."

Papa continued, "I am always trying to think of ways to keep them from stealing seeds from my feeders and they outsmart me every time. Their little brains must be just one *bag full of tricks.*"

"They won't steal our seeds," said Lucy confidently. "I'll guard our feeder and chase them away every time they show up and I'll steal their bag with the tricks inside."

"Looks like they are *getting Lucy's goat* already," said Papa. "We need to put our heads together, *put on our thinking caps* and come up with a plan to get Mr. Squirrel's goat."

First, let's watch Mr. Squirrel and see how he gets at the seeds. Then we'll try to think of a way to stop him."

"I don't have a goat," said Lucy, "but if I did, I'll bet Mr. Squirrel couldn't steal it from me."

"It's just another one of those old sayings," explained Papa. "If you had a pet goat and someone stole it, I'm sure that would make you mad."

They didn't have to sit at the window very long before a squirrel came bouncing across the lawn. It stopped right under the feeder and looked up.

"They may have a tiny brain," said Papa, "but I've been outsmarted by them more times than I can count. You can just tell this guy's figuring out the best way to get at those seeds."

The squirrel would tilt its head one way, then another. Every few seconds it would stop and scratch rapidly. The girls started laughing as the squirrel would look, then scratch behind its ear. Then it would look up every few seconds and scratch again somewhere else. This went on for several minutes. His little paws were moving *a mile a minute.*

The girls were enjoying the show. Harper came over to the window to see what was happening. She wasn't sure but soon was laughing right along with everyone else.

"Looks like the fleas are having breakfast too," said Papa.

"I thought Tillie was the only one with fleas," said Delainey.

"Any animal that has fur will also have little visitors," said Papa. "It's only fair—they take our seeds and the fleas take a little squirrel meat."

Suddenly the squirrel jumped straight up in the air and came down on its back, rubbing up and down along the grass.

"I think those fleas are making Mr. Squirrel crazy," said Papa. "He looks like *he's at the end of his rope.*"

"I don't see any rope," said Lucy.

"All right," said Papa. *"He's at his wit's end."*

"What?" asked Delainey.

"It just means he can't figure out how to stop what's bothering him, and it's driving him cuckoo," said Papa.

The squirrel stopped to scratch still another place, then bounded down the hill and headed for the creek as fast as his little legs could carry him.

"I'll bet he's going to take a bath in the creek and try to wash off the fleas," said Delainey.

They all had a good laugh at the bushy-tailed thief's expense.

"He's got more on his mind than seeds right now," said Papa. "I guess we're going to have to wait for another time to see if we can save our seeds from Mr. Squirrel."

"Good," said Lucy. "I hope those fleas got *his* goat."

THE FISHING TRIP

Papa thought it was time for the girls to learn to fish. "How would you girls like to go on a fishing trip to Whitesburg Pond?" asked Papa. He appeared with his arms full of strange-looking things.

"Is that what those sticks are for?" asked Lucy.

"These are fishing poles I put together for you, and I brought a lot more *paraphernalia* needed if you want to catch fish," answered Papa.

"What's para….paranaila and why do we need it to catch fish?" asked Delainey.

Their grandpa smiled. "It's just another name for a bunch of stuff. We need stuff like bobbers to tell us when a fish is on the line, sinkers to weigh the lines down and hooks for the bait to catch the fish. Then you need to learn how to use it if you're going to be a good fisherman."

"I hope we can catch some for supper," said Delainey. "I like fish."

"Me, too," echoed Lucy. "They're even better than the fish sticks Grandma makes when we stay over."

"Sorry, but we can't keep what we catch there," said Papa. "It is a rule that fish have to go back in the pond so other boys and girls can have the fun of catching them too. It is such a small pond that if everyone kept them, pretty soon they'd be *few and far between*. They'd become *scarce as hen's teeth*.

"I know, Papa," said Delainey proudly. "Hens don't even have teeth. If there were no fish in the pond, no one could go fishing there with their daddy or their grandpa."

"Right you are," said Papa. "Then everyone would have to *pull up stakes* and find another fishing hole."

"What are they using stakes for?" asked Lucy. "Do they fish with them?"

"No, laughed Papa. "It's just another one of my old sayings.

Long ago people lived in tents, and when they moved they had to pull out the tent stakes so they could set up somewhere else."

"That's silly, Papa," said Lucy. "Did you make that up to tease us? Why did people live in tents? Why don't they live in houses?"

"That was a long time ago before houses were invented," explained Papa, hoping that explanation would satisfy her.

"Can we go fishing right now, Papa?" asked Delainey.

"Sure, and I even brought along some night crawlers for bait and my camera for pictures of your catches," said Papa.

"What's a night crawler?" asked Lucy.

"It's just a name for a big worm. They live deep under ground and only come out at night. You have to walk around the lawn after dark with a flashlight and look for them lying in the grass. They are hard to catch because they move quickly back in their hole and they are as *slippery as an eel*."

"What's an eel and why is it slippery, Papa?" asked Delainey.

"An eel is a long, skinny fish almost like a snake except it's real slimy and hard to hold," explained Papa.

"Yuck! Who would want to hold them?" asked Lucy.

"I don't blame you," said Papa. "They are very ugly, but some people like to eat them."

"Double Yuck!" said Lucy. "I'm never going to eat any. I hope we don't catch any when we go fishing today."

"I'm pretty certain you won't have to worry about that at Whitesburg Pond, Lucy," said Papa. "Now pile in the car and buckle up. Let's go catch some fish!" Papa knew he wouldn't have time to fish. He'd be busy putting worms on hooks and, hopefully, taking pictures and putting fish back in the pond.

It was a short drive across town to Whitesburg Park.

"We're very lucky to have a nice park like this so close to town," said Papa. "It's so pretty and peaceful."

The girls got out of the car and rushed over to the edge of the pond. As they looked across the water, ripples appeared on the smooth surface.

"Are those fish making trails in the water, Papa?" asked Delainey.

"They sure are. Let me bait your hooks so you can *get down to brass tacks* and catch some nice fat bluegills."

"These don't look like tacks," said Lucy. "How could a worm stay on a tack anyway?"

"It just means we have to get down to business. The worm will stay on the hook unless you *fall asleep at the switch,* or I mean the pole, and let them steal your bait," said Papa. "The bobber will float, but when it starts dancing it tells you a fish is thinking about having your worm for lunch. I know it's tempting, but don't pull on your line until the bobber goes under the water and starts moving."

Grandpa tossed their lines into the water and handed the girls a pole.

"Now you have to stay *bright eyed and bushy-tailed*—I mean stay alert, because there should be a nibble at your bait in about *two shakes of a lamb's tail.*"

There was no time to ask what that meant because it took less time than *two shakes of a lamb's tail* before Lucy's bobber started dancing. She quickly pulled her line out of the water, but there was nothing but an empty hook.

"Oh no!" she moaned. "The fish stole my worm."

"Don't get *bent out of shape* and upset over this. No sense *crying over spilled milk*," said Papa.

"What?" asked Lucy. How can losing a fish be like the milk I spilled at breakfast today?"

"Well, Lucy," explained Papa, "you didn't get *bent out of shape*, or I mean upset, because you knew there was more milk. You lost a fish out there but there is no sense getting upset over it because there will be more fish to catch. Next time you can try again and be more careful. Wait a little longer so the fish has time to take the hook and the worm in its mouth. Remember, wait till the bobber goes under the water and starts moving. Most people have an *itchy trigger finger* the first time they fish, and they pull the bobber up too soon."

Delainey was more interested in watching Lucy. "What's that mean?" she asked.

Papa explained, "When someone has an *itchy trigger finger* that means they shoot off a gun before they take careful aim. Then they usually miss their target. So it means you were too anxious and rushed to catch the fish before it was hooked."

Papa glanced over at Delainey's line. "Where's your bobber, Delainey?" he asked. Just then it popped up on the surface out in the middle of the pond. Delainey had a look of panic on her face and she ran away from shore, pulling the line up on the bank.

"Oh no!" she moaned. "The fish stole my worm too."

"It's O.K.," said Papa. "I hope you both learned a lesson. Lucy didn't wait long enough and you waited too long. You have to pull at just the right time."

Grandpa baited their hooks once more. "I'll *bet my britches* and *I'll eat my hat* if you don't catch a fish this time. Remember…"

"We know," the girls interrupted. "Wait till the bobber goes under and starts to move and then yank on the line."

Almost immediately both bobbers disappeared. The girls gave the line a quick tug and each pulled a fat bluegill up on the bank. Papa quickly grabbed each fish as it flopped around on the shore.

"Hold the fish up so I can take a picture for Mama and Daddy," said Papa. "Then we will let them go. Now they are free to provide fun for other boys and girls."

The girls both squealed with glee. "Now Papa won't lose his pants," said Delainey.

"And he won't have to eat his hat either," chimed in Lucy. "Now that we know how, we'll never lose our bait to a fish again."

"I wouldn't *bet my britches* on that," laughed Papa.

A DAY ON THE SLEDDING HILL

The girls were very lucky. A great sled-riding hill was right in their own back yard. They only had to walk a few steps and there it was—the hill was just waiting for them. The only thing missing was enough snow to cover the ground.

The girls were excited because Daddy told them that the weather report said that a heavy snowfall was expected overnight. They were sure they would wake up to a fresh blanket of snow because their Daddy was always right.

"Lu, Lu, wake up—come look out the window," said Delainey. Her excitement meant only one thing. Sure enough, huge white flakes filled the air and had already covered the ground.

"Hooray!" shouted Delainey. "Now we can go sled riding. I'm sure there will be plenty of snow."

Lucy was not as excited as her older sister. She had watched the other kids enjoy sliding down the hill, but was still unsure of trying it herself. She even resisted when Daddy offered to ride down with her. Whenever Lucy would get up the nerve, she'd look down the steep slope and move off to the rear of the line of eager sledders waiting their turn.

"Come on, Lu. Let's get our snowsuits on and go outside. It'll be fun—wait and see!" Delainey's words of encouragement seemed to work for the moment.

The girls scampered down the stairs to the kitchen. It was Saturday so Daddy would be home all day.

"Not so fast," said Mama. "You act like you've got *ants in your pants*. Snowsuits come on <u>after</u> breakfast."

Delainey was too excited to eat, but she knew what came first so she sat down and waited. Harper was well into her second helping of scrambled eggs. It seemed like every time Mama turned around her tray was empty. Daddy brought over two plates of freshly scrambled eggs for the girls. Delainey's eyes were not on the eggs, but on the hillside where several neighborhood children were already enjoying the fresh snow.

Suddenly a familiar face appeared at the kitchen window.

"Look, it's Papa!" shouted Delainey. "He's come over to go sledding with us." Both girls rushed over to the window to greet their grandpa through the glass. Papa breathed on the window and wrote "I ♥ You!" on the misty glass. Then he motioned for them to come outside.

"I guess that's it for breakfast, but you have to finish your eggs first," said Daddy. "Then we'll all go outside."

Soon the girls were dressed in their snowsuits and were out the back door with their daddy. Harper remained inside with her nose pressed against the steamy window.

Delainey grabbed her dad's hand and rushed over to her grandpa.

"Papa, you came over to sled with us. Daddy said we'd have a snow day."

Lucy came over to greet her grandpa but stood behind him, not looking at the hill.

"Let's go, Daddy," said Delainey. "The kids are having such fun."

Although the hill was not long, it was very steep so that sledders picked up enough speed to travel all the way across the lower lawn right up to the edge of the creek.

Dad looked at Papa. "Maybe you can talk Lucy into riding down with you. We haven't been able to get her to take that first ride yet."

"Is that right, Lucy?" said Papa. "Let me tell you a story about what happened to me when I was right about your age. We had a very big hill right next to our backyard. It was the best hill in town and kids came from everywhere to go sledding. There was even a big barrel with a blazing fire to warm our hands. I would go over every day to watch. I even dragged my sled out, but I never went near the hill. After awhile the kids noticed I wouldn't go down the hill and they called me a *stick-in-the mud.*"

"What's a *stick-in-the- mud*?" asked Lucy.

"Well," said Papa, "it's a person who stands around watching other people having fun but won't join in. They stay where they are as if their feet were stuck in the mud. Each day I watched everyone else having such a good time. Finally I said to myself, 'If everyone is having so much fun, why am I just standing here'? No one else was afraid but me. Finally I got up enough courage and I asked one of the older kids if I could ride down with him on the back of his sled. Every day I stood there with my sled, *like a bump on a log,* and never used it.

"That's a silly thing to be, " said Lucy. "Whoever heard of someone being a *bump on a log?"*

"It just means you are there but not doing a single thing," explained Papa.

"I was afraid to take that first ride, but after it was over I realized what fun I had been missing all that time."

Lucy looked up at Papa and said, "Will you ride down with me, Papa? I don't want to be a *stick-in-the-mud* anymore."

From that day on, Lucy enjoyed the sledding hill as much as everyone else and she was never a *stick in the mud* or *a bump on a log* again.

ACKNOWLEDGMENTS

About two years ago Dale Slavin, a noted local artist, approached me about the possibility of illustrating a children's book. I was flattered, but at that time nothing was in the works. Some time later an idea for the book began to materialize, and I asked Dale if he was still interested. When I explained my idea, his enthusiasm gave me the incentive to begin in earnest. I feel very fortunate to have Dale contributing his artistic skill to this effort.

Ron Humphrey of Windjammer Adventure Publishing was another person on whom I relied heavily. Ron and I had collaborated on a book I had done earlier. Without his expertise, guidance and patience, this book would never have come to fruition.

Finally, my wife Marilyn's secretarial skills filled a void that allowed this book to translate from unintelligible scribbles into meaningful sentences. She has been an integral part of the books I have previously written. Without her, I could have never benefited from the skills of Dale and Ron.